Cesar Chavez

Terry Barber

ACTIVIST
SERIES

Cesar Chavez is published by
Grass Roots Press, a division of Literacy Services of Canada Ltd.

PHONE 1–888–303–3213
WEBSITE www.grassrootsbooks.net

ACKNOWLEDGEMENTS

We acknowledge the financial support of the Government of Canada through the
Book Publishing Industry Development Program (BPIDP) for our publishing activities.

We acknowledge the support of
the Alberta Foundation for the Arts
for our publishing programs.

Editor: Dr. Pat Campbell
Image Research: Dr. Pat Campbell
Book design: Lara Minja, Lime Design Inc.

Library and Archives Canada Cataloguing in Publication

Barber, Terry, date
      Cesar Chavez / Terry Barber.

(Activist series)
ISBN 978–1–894593–51–9

      1. Readers for new literates. 2. Chavez, Cesar, 1927–. 3. Labor
leaders—United States—Biography. I. Title. II. Series.

HD6509.C48B37 2006   428.6'2   C2006–903722–1

Printed in Canada

Contents

People walk with the coffin of Cesar Chavez.

A Hero Dies

It is 1993. Cesar Chavez dies in his sleep. He dies in peace. More than 40,000 people go to his funeral. They go to say goodbye. They are saying goodbye to a hero. Cesar has spent his life helping farm workers.

These children must read English.

Early Years

Cesar Chavez is Mexican-American. He speaks and reads Spanish at home. At school, Cesar must speak and read English. He gets hit for speaking Spanish. Cesar does not like school.

Cesar was born on March 31, 1927. He is the second of six children.

Cesar and his sister stand outside their home.

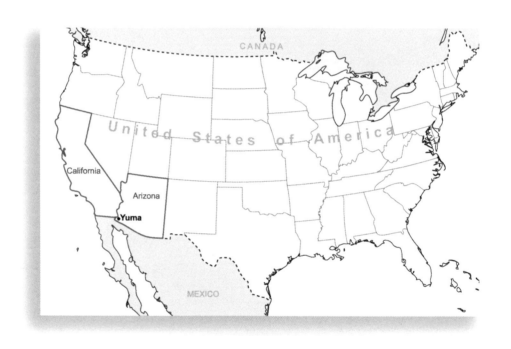

The Chavez family owns a farm in Yuma, Arizona.

Early Years

The Chavez family owns a farm in Arizona. But hard times come. In 1937, the Chavez family loses the farm. Cesar's father becomes a **migrant** farm worker. They move to California.

The Chavez family loses its farm during the Great Depression.

This family moves from farm to farm.

Early Years

Migrant farm workers move from farm to farm. They move to find work. They plant and pick crops on fields. Then, they move to a new farm. The Chavez family works on many farms. The Chavez family moves all over California.

More than 250,000 migrant workers live in California.

Cesar and his family sit by their car.

These farm workers pick lettuce.

Early Years

The Chavez family pick many crops.
In winter, they pick lettuce. In spring,
they pick beans. In summer, they pick
grapes. In fall, they pick cotton.

This child picks spinach.

Early Years

The children must work in the fields. They miss a lot of school. Cesar goes to more than 30 schools. Many of the teachers and children are **racist.** Some children call Cesar a "dirty Mexican."

Some of the schools are **segregated.**

This worker's home is by a field.

The Migrant Farmer's Life

Some farm workers live in shacks. The shacks do not have toilets or running water. The rent is very high. The rent is taken from their pay.

Others live in tents. Some sleep in cars and trucks. Some sleep under the stars.

This family lives in a tent.

This is the only food in her home.

The Migrant Farmer's Life

The farm workers' lives are hard. They work long hours. The farm workers make little money. It is hard to buy food. It is hard to find clean water to drink. It is hard to find clean water for washing.

A migrant farmer works in the fields.

Cesar Joins the Work Force

One day, Cesar's father has a car accident. He cannot work in the fields anymore. Cesar needs to support his family. He leaves school. Cesar works in the fields for two years.

Cesar holds his Grade 8 diploma, 1942.

Cesar Chavez leaves school after Grade 8. He is 15 years old.

A U.S. Navy poster, 1944.

Cesar Joins the Work Force

In 1944, Cesar joins the U.S. Navy.
He wants to escape life in the fields.
He serves in the navy during World
War II. Cesar is only 17.

Cesar
Chavez serves
in the navy for
two years.

Cesar in his
U.S. Navy uniform.

Cesar and Helen on their honeymoon.

Cesar and Helen with six of their children, 1968.

Cesar Joins the Work Force

After the war, Cesar marries Helen.
His wife is also from a family of
migrant workers. It is hard for Cesar
to find work. He has little education.
Cesar goes back to working in the
fields.

Cesar marries Helen Fabela in 1948. They have eight children.

Cesar helps farm workers vote.

Cesar Joins the Work Force

In 1952, Cesar gets a new job.
He works for a civil rights group.
He farms all day and works for the
group at night. He teaches **Latino**
people about their rights. Cesar helps
Latino people learn how to vote.

The civil rights group is called the Community Service Organization.

A 32-year-old migrant farmer with her child.

Union Leader

In the 1950s, farm workers' lives are still hard. They have little hope of a better life. Cesar wants to give his people hope. He wants to see change. He wants better pay. He wants better living conditions. He wants better working conditions.

Cesar talks with his assistant in front
of the union building.

Union Leader

Cesar moves to Delano, California. In 1962, he forms a union. Cesar is the president. The union **unites** the farmers. The union wants farm workers to have a better life.

The union is called the National Farm Worker's Association.

This woman holds the union's flag.

Union Leader

The union has a flag. The flag is red, white, and black. The black eagle stands for the worker's problems. The white circle stands for hope. The red stands for hard work. The flag is the union's **symbol.**

Cesar walks with union members.

Union Leader

Farm workers begin to join the union.
The workers want the farm owners to
treat them better. By 1965, over 1200
people join the union. More and more
people join the union. The union gives
them more power.

Cesar leads a banana boycott.

Union Leader

Cesar believes in peaceful protests. He believes these protests can lead to change. Cesar goes on hunger strikes. He leads marches. Cesar leads strikes. He leads **boycotts.**

Cesar sits in front of two of his heros—
Gandhi and Robert Kennedy.

Union Leader

Cesar does not believe in violence. His heroes include Martin Luther King and Mahatma Gandhi. These two men do not believe in violence. They believe that peaceful ways can bring change.

Cesar leads a grape boycott.

Union Leader

In 1965, grape growers cut their workers' pay. The union **protests** the pay cut. Cesar leads a grape boycott. People stop buying grapes.

Union workers go on strike. They walk off the grape fields.

Over 13 million Americans support the grape boycott.

Cesar signs a contract that ends the grape strike.

Union Leader

The grape strike ends in 1970. Cesar and the grape growers sign a contract.

The contract is good for migrant farm workers. Their pay is better. Working conditions are better. Farm workers hold their heads higher. Cesar has helped make their lives better.

Paul Chavez stands by a stamp of his father, Cesar Chavez.

A Special Person

Cesar dies in 1993. People remember him as a special person. Cesar gets many honours. Schools are named after Cesar. Parks are named after Cesar. Streets are named after Cesar. He spent his life helping farm workers.

President Bill Clinton awards Cesar Chavez the Medal of Freedom in 1994. His wife, Helen Chavez, accepts the award.

Glossary

boycott: to refuse to use a service or buy a product.

Latino: a Latin American person who lives in the United States.

migrant: a person who moves from one place to another.

protest: to complain about something.

racist: a belief that one race is superior to others.

segregate: to separate a race or class from other people.

symbol: a picture that stands for an idea.

unite: to bring or join together.

Talking About the Book

What did you learn about Cesar Chavez?

What did you learn about migrant farm workers?

Do you think a boycott is a good way to protest? Why or why not?

How did Cesar Chavez make the lives of others better?

Picture Credits